LET'S EXPLORE SCIENCE

Air & Flying

David Evans and Claudette Williams

DK

DORLING KINDERSLEY
LONDON • NEW YORK • STUTTGART

A DORLING KINDERSLEY BOOK

Project Editor Stella Love
Art Editor Sara Nunan
Designer Cheryl Telfer
Managing Editor Jane Yorke
Managing Art Editor Chris Scollen
Production Jayne Wood
Photography by Susanna Price
U.S. Assistant Editor Lara Tankel

First American Edition, 1993
2 4 6 8 10 9 7 5 3 1

Published in the United States by
Dorling Kindersley, Inc., 232 Madison Avenue
New York, New York 10016

Copyright © 1993
Dorling Kindersley Limited, London

Library of Congress Cataloging-in-Publication Data

Evans, David. 1937-
  Air and flying / by David Evans and Claudette Williams. -- 1st
American ed.
      p. cm. -- (Let's explore science)
  Includes index.
  Summary: Includes activities that explore the properties of air,
such as how it feels, how it moves, and how it keeps things airborne.
  ISBN 1-56458-343-0
  1. Aerodynamics--Juvenile literature. 2. Aerodynamics-
-Experiments--Juvenile literature. 3. Flight--Juvenile literature.
4. Flight--Experiments--Juvenile literature. [1. Air--Experiments.
2. Aerodynamics--Experiments. 3. Experiments.] I. Williams,
Claudette. II. Title. III. Series.
TL570.E79 1993   93-3156
621.132'3--dc20   CIP
                                                           AC

Reproduced by J. Film Process Singapore Pte., Ltd.
Printed and bound in Belgium by Proost

Dorling Kindersley would like to thank the following for their help in
producing this book: Dave King and Kim Taylor (for additional photography);
Coral Mula (for safety symbol artwork); Mark Richards (for jacket design);
and the Franklin Delano Roosevelt School, London.
Dorling Kindersley would also like to give special thanks to the following for
appearing in this book: Natalie Agada; Hannah Capleton; Gregory Coleman;
Karen Edwards; Sapphire Elia; Sophia El Kaddar; Howard Jones;
Tony Locke; Gemma Loke; Maxwell Ralph; and Anthony Singh.

Contents

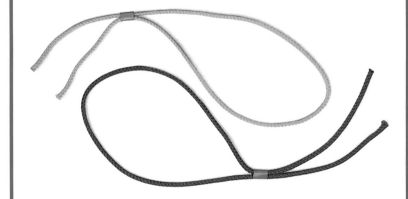

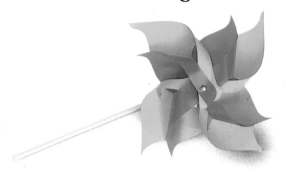
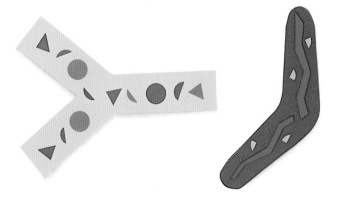

Note to parents and teachers

Young children are forever asking questions about the things they see, touch, hear, smell, and taste.

The **Let's Explore Science** series aims to foster children's natural curiosity and encourages them to use their senses to find out about science. Each book features a variety of experiments based on one topic, which draw on a young child's everyday experiences. By investigating familiar activities, such as bouncing a ball, making cookies, or clapping hands, young children will learn that science plays an important part in the world around them.

Investigative approach

Young children can only begin to understand science if they are stimulated to think and find out for themselves. For these reasons, an open-ended questioning approach is used in the **Let's Explore Science** books and, wherever possible, results of experiments are not shown. Children are encouraged to make their own scientific discoveries and to interpret them according to their own ideas. This investigative approach to learning makes science exciting and not just about acquiring "facts." This way of learning will assist children in many areas of their education.

Using the books

Before starting an experiment, check the text and pictures to ensure that you have gathered any necessary equipment. Allow children to help in this process and to suggest alternative materials to use. Once ready, it is important to let children decide how to carry out the experiment and what the result means to them. You can help by asking questions, such as, "What do you think will happen?" or "What did you do?"

Household equipment

All the experiments can be carried out easily at home. In most cases, inexpensive household objects and materials are used.

Guide to experiments

The *Guide to experiments* on pages 28-29 is intended to help parents, teachers, or helpers using this book with children. It gives an outline of the scientific principles underlying the experiments, includes useful tips for carrying out the activities, suggests alternative equipment to use, and additional activities to try.

Safe experimenting

This symbol appears next to experiments where children may require adult supervision or assistance, such as, when they are heating things or using sharp tools.

About this book

Air and Flying challenges young children to detect the presence of air and gases and to investigate the physical properties of air. The activities lead children to explore how different shapes fly or fall in the air, how air can be moved, and how moving air can be used to propel objects. The experiments enable children to discover that:

- air is all around us and although we cannot see, taste, or smell it, we can feel it;
- air has mass and moves to fill spaces;
- air contains oxygen that allows combustion (burning);
- when air is heated it will expand and when it is cooled it will contract;
- when air is compressed, e.g., pumped into a balloon, it will exert a force;
- forces can move air and the movement can be detected as wind;
- some shapes will move through air with less resistance than others;
- air contains gases that support life and is therefore essential to living things;
- air can be polluted and some forms of pollution can be seen.

With your help, young children will enjoy exploring the world of science and discover that finding out is fun.

David Evans and Claudette Williams

9

Can you feel the air?

What do you feel or see when
you try these experiments?

Umbrella
What do you feel
when you push and
pull an open umbrella
in front of you?

Does it feel the
same when you
close the umbrella?

Bag
Can you feel the air
when you wave your
hand? What will
happen if you put
a paper bag over one
hand and wave again?

Squeeze bottle
What happens when you squeeze a dish-washing liquid bottle filled with air? Does it feel the same with the top open?

Balloon
What does air escaping from a balloon feel like? Which part of your body feels air the best?

Streamer
What will air do to a streamer on a windy day?

Where is the air?

Can you tell where the air is as you try each of these experiments?

Bubbles

Can you trap air in soap bubbles? Mix some dish-washing liquid with water and dip a loop of rope into it. How can you get the air out of the bubbles?

Straw

What do you see if you blow through a straw into some water? Where is the air?

Carbonated water

Go outside and shake a bottle of carbonated water. Point the top away from you and take the top off. What will happen?

Funnel and bottle

With modeling clay, seal a funnel into the top of a plastic bottle.

What happens when you quickly pour some water into the funnel?

Paper bag

Blow up a paper bag. What is inside it? What will happen if you burst the bag with your hands?

Brick

What do you see when you put a brick into water? What happens when you put a bottle without a top into water?

Make a hole in the side of the bottle. Now what will happen when you pour water into the funnel again?

15

Will it stay in the air?

What kinds of things can you make stay up in the air?

Ball and straw
Blow through a bent straw. Can you make a table-tennis ball hover in the air?

Paper
Will a flat sheet of paper stay in the air for longer than a scrunched-up sheet of paper?

What will happen if you drop a big sheet of paper and a small sheet of paper at the same time?

Feather
How can you keep a feather in the air?

Whirligig

Ask an adult to help you make a whirligig. Cut out a cardboard wing like this. Push a stick through the middle of the cardboard.

Roll the stick between your hands to make it spin quickly, and then let go. Will the whirligig stay up in the air?

Balloon

For how long can you keep a balloon up in the air?

What will happen if you make the cardboard wing bigger?

Will it fly in the air?

Make a hot-air balloon and a kite.
Can you make them fly up into the air?

Hot-air balloon
Cut out six large
pieces of tissue paper
shaped like this.

To make a paper
balloon, glue each
piece of tissue
paper to the next
along one edge.

What will
happen if
you fill the paper
balloon with hot
air from a hair
dryer and
let go?

Kite

Can you make a paper kite with a large square of paper?

Fold the paper like this.

Tape a piece of thread from one corner to the other to make a bridle.

Ask an adult to help you tie the loose end of a spool of thread onto the bridle to make the kite string. Now cut out and stick on a strip of paper to make a tail.

Kite flying

How high will your kite fly? How long will it stay up in the air?

kite string

tail

Is the air clean?

What things need clean air?
How can you find out if the
air where you live is clean?

Birds

Can you see any birds in
the sky? Do they fly by
gliding or by flapping
their wings?

People

Where does
air go into
your body?

Insects

Can you find some
insects outside?
Which ones
have wings
and can fly?

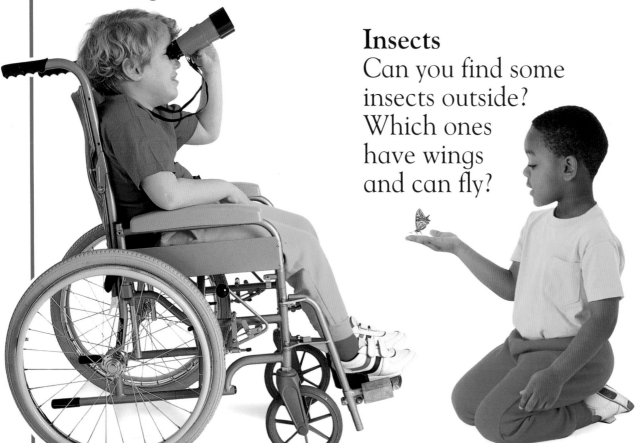

Which parts
of your body
move when
you breathe
in or out?

Paper
Spread a sheet of white paper outside and leave some things on it for a few days.

What will you see when you go back and lift up the things?

Mask
Wear a mask when you ride a bicycle. After a long time, look at the mask. How does it look different from a new mask?

What has made the mask change?

Index

Guide to experiments

The notes below briefly outline the scientific principles underlying the experiments and include suggestions for alternative equipment to use and activities to try.

Can you feel the air? 10-11

These activities make children aware of the presence of air around them as they feel it against their bodies and other objects. The umbrella and paper bag make large surfaces against which the resistance of the air can be felt. Looking at a streamer on a windy day introduces the idea of air moving as wind.

What is air like? 12-13

Air has mass and is heavy and this is shown by balancing two deflated balloons and then inflating one of them. Children should be supervised as they experiment to find out that oxygen in the air is needed to keep things burning. Putting balloons in warm and cold places will show that air expands and contracts. The paper snake will detect the movement of warm air.

Where is the air? 14-15

The experiments to trap air in soap solution, blow bubbles into water or release the gas in a carbonated drink will help children realize that air and other invisible gases exist. Trapping air in a paper bag or watching air bubbles escape from a brick in water will develop this awareness. Water will not go into a sealed bottle of air unless the air can be pushed out of the bottle through a small hole.

Can you make air move? 16-17

Children can investigate the effects of making air move through sucking, blowing, or fanning. Blowing air through a reed pipe causes air to vibrate and a sound is produced. Blowing between two sheets of paper reduces the pressure between them. The surrounding air pressure pushes the sheets together.

Will it stay in the air? 18-19

The air offers resistance to falling objects and the larger the surface in contact with the air, the slower the descent will be. The table-tennis ball will hover in the air for as long as the air current continues, but the feather can be kept in the air with intermittent puffs of air because its rate of descent is slow. The wing of the whirligig acts like a helicopter wing, creating an upward force which balances the force of gravity pulling the wing to the ground.

Will it fly or fall? 20-21

Children are challenged to make more devices to propel through the air and to find ways to delay their descent. The shape of boomerangs gives them a bias as they fly, which makes them turn in the air. Further activities could include making and testing paper airplanes.

Will it fly in the air? 22-23

When air becomes warm, it becomes less dense than the surrounding air and starts to rise. Children harness this principle in making a hot-air balloon out of very light paper. The kite shown is simple to make and flies well, but other shapes or materials could also be tried.

Will air make it go? 22-23

Moving air is used to propel objects. The blow rocket requires a puff of air from the lungs which may be a problem for children with asthma. Air escaping from a balloon pushes against the surrounding air and this drives the rocket and boats.

Is the air clean? 26-27

Children are asked to think about creatures that use the air and then about our need for clean air. Using a gauze face mask or leaving a sheet of paper outside will reveal that there are dirt and dust particles in the air.

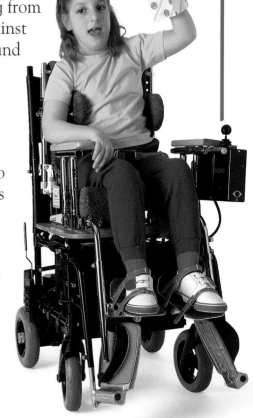

29